BRIGHT IDEA BOOKS

PET Groomer

by Marie Pearson

CAPSTONE PRESS
a capstone imprint

Bright Idea Books are published by Capstone Press
1710 Roe Crest Drive, North Mankato, Minnesota 56003
www.mycapstone.com

Library of Congress Cataloging-in-Publication Data
Names: Pearson, Marie, author.
Title: Pet groomer / by Marie Pearson.
Description: North Mankato, Minnesota : Bright Idea Books, an imprint of
   Capstone Press, [2019] | Series: Jobs with animals | Audience: Age 9-12. |
   Audience: Grade 4 to 6. | Includes bibliographical references and index.
Identifiers: LCCN 2018035989 | ISBN 9781543557879 (hardcover : alk. paper) |
   ISBN 9781543558197 (ebook) | ISBN 9781543560497 (paperback)
Subjects: LCSH: Pet grooming salons--Vocational guidance--Juvenile
   literature. | Dog grooming industry--Vocational guidance--Juvenile
   literature.
Classification: LCC SF427.55 .P43 2019 | DDC 636.7/0833--dc23
LC record available at https://lccn.loc.gov/2018035989

Editorial Credits
Editor: Meg Gaertner
Designer: Becky Daum
Production Specialist: Dan Peluso

Photo Credits
iStockphoto: 2002lubava1981, 6, andriano_cz, 8–9, Darunechka, 14–15, LuckyBusiness, 23, ollegN, 11, Ranta Images, 27, Thepalmer, 30–31; Shutterstock Images: A_Lesik, 26, Anton Gvozdikov, 12–13, Eric Isselee, 17, 28, Ligfo, 9, LightField Studios, cover, nazarovsergey, 20–21, Nomad_Soul, 19, rodimov, 24, sirtravelalot, 5, Susan Schmitz, 6–7, Tinxi, 16–17

Printed in the United States of America.
PA48

TABLE OF CONTENTS

CHAPTER 1

PET
Groomer

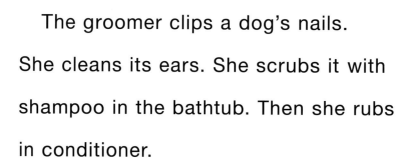

The groomer clips a dog's nails. She cleans its ears. She scrubs it with shampoo in the bathtub. Then she rubs in conditioner.

The groomer lifts the dog to the drying table. She uses a blow dryer. It dries and loosens fur.

Groomers wash pets in special tubs.

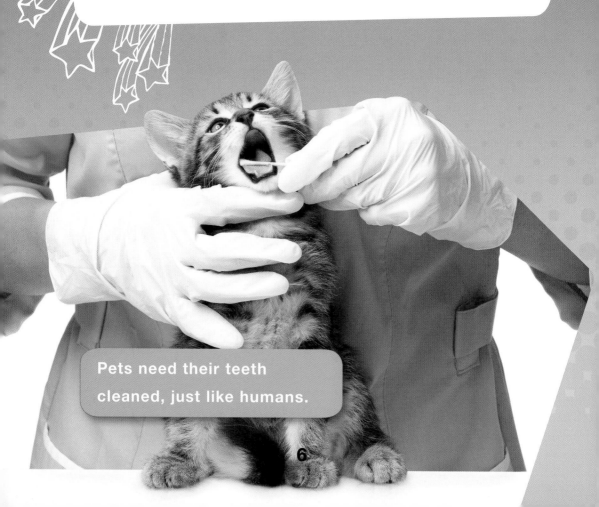

The groomer brings the dog to the grooming table. She brushes the dog. This helps it shed less. She shaves the fur between its paw pads. She trims its ear hair. The dog's bottom also gets shaved. This helps it stay clean.

Pets need their teeth cleaned, just like humans.

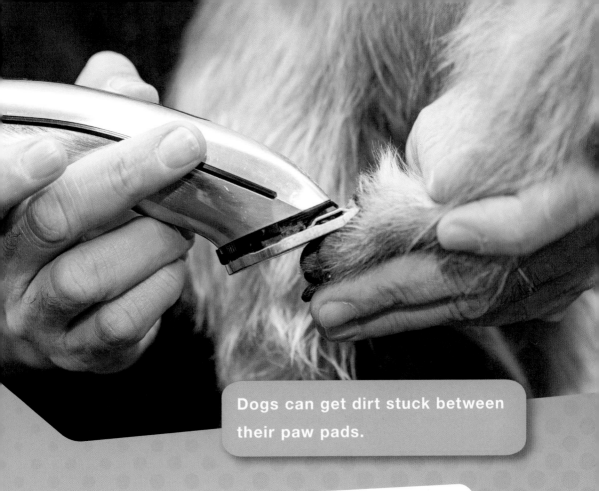

Dogs can get dirt stuck between their paw pads.

Groomers have many tasks. They brush teeth. They give full haircuts. Some groomers dye fur in fun colors. They might paint dogs' nails.

Groomers remove ticks from dogs' ears and fur.

Groomers usually groom dogs and cats. But they might also work with rabbits or other **species**. Some groomers work with only one species.

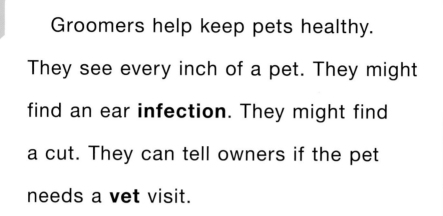

Groomers help keep pets healthy. They see every inch of a pet. They might find an ear **infection**. They might find a cut. They can tell owners if the pet needs a **vet** visit.

Bunnies sometimes need to get their nails clipped.

9

CHAPTER 2

QUALITIES AND Skills

Groomers love animals. Many groomers work with all kinds of pets every day. They are confident around all pets.

Groomers are patient and kind.
Pets wiggle. They shake and bite.
Being patient can help calm pets.
Groomers are also careful. They use
sharp tools. These tools could cut
active pets.

Not all pets enjoy
getting baths. Groomers
must be careful so they
do not get scratched.

Groomers handle every inch
of dogs' thick coats.

A MESSY JOB

Groomers can handle gross things. Some dogs have poop in their bottoms. Others have eye boogers. The groomer has to clean them off. Sometimes there are bugs in a dog's thick coat.

STRENGTH NEEDED

Groomers need to be strong. They lift pets. Some dogs weigh more than 200 pounds (90 kilograms).

Groomers know how to care for all fur types. Some owners do not groom their dogs enough. Dogs may come in with long, **matted** fur. Groomers know how to safely shave off mats without cutting the animal.

WORKING WITH OWNERS

Groomers have good communication skills. They work with pet owners. They need to understand what owners want. Sometimes owners get upset. Groomers need to be calm and polite. They should be honest if they made a mistake.

Groomers shave mats out of fur instead of cutting them out. This helps keep the animal from being injured.

Groomers sometimes use special hair spray to keep a dog's fur fluffy and full.

Groomers know how to make pets look good. Different breeds of dogs get different haircuts. Good groomers know each one. They can also do fun haircuts. Owners might want a dog to have a Mohawk.

COMPETITIONS

Some groomers compete in grooming competitions. They style dogs carefully. They even make dogs look like other animals.

Some owners want their pets to be colorful.

CHAPTER 3

THE
Workplace

Groomers are needed anywhere there are pets. They work many places. Some work in grooming **salons**. These businesses specialize in grooming pets.

Others work at boarding kennels or vet clinics. Groomers might also work from home.

Grooming salons have all the tools groomers need to clean pets.

Groomers use many different tools in their work.

Some groomers travel to clients in a special van. The van has a tub and a water tank. It has everything groomers need to groom pets.

THE PAY

Groomers generally make between $19,000 and $37,000 per year. Some get paid by the hour. Some make a **percentage** of the cost of grooming. Groomers usually take **tips**.

BRUSHES

There is a different brush for every type of fur. Some brushes are only good for short fur. Pet groomers know when to use each type of brush.

CHAPTER 4

EDUCATION

Groomers do not need to go to college. But they should have experience handling animals. They should know animal **behavior**. This helps them handle pets safely.

24

GETTING EXPERIENCE

Groomers get experience in many ways. Some people take online classes. Others go to school. Students learn by handling real pets. They learn about different breeds. They learn how to care for all fur types.

Some students work as **apprentices**. They watch and help a groomer. The groomer teaches them the skills they need.

Pets leave the salon
looking their best.

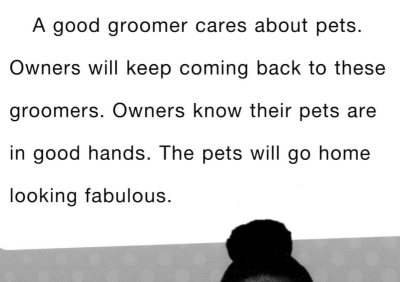

A good groomer cares about pets. Owners will keep coming back to these groomers. Owners know their pets are in good hands. The pets will go home looking fabulous.

Pets with clean, unmatted fur are more enjoyable to pet and handle.

GLOSSARY

apprentice
a person learning a job from someone already skilled in that job

behavior
the way in which a living being acts

infection
a disease from bacteria

matted
tangled together tightly

percentage
a portion of the full amount

salon
a business that provides grooming services for pets

species
a group of plants or animals of the same kind that can produce offspring together

tip
money given in addition to the cost of a service

vet
a doctor who takes care of animals

OTHER JOBS TO CONSIDER

BOARDING KENNEL WORKER

Many dogs stay at a kennel when their owners are away. Boarding kennel workers take care of them. The workers feed the dogs and provide them with exercise.

DOG WALKER

Some owners are not able to walk their dogs. They hire a dog walker. Dog walkers may walk many dogs at once. They help dogs get exercise.

PET SITTER

Some animals stay at home while their owners are away. The owners hire pet sitters to take care of them. Pet sitters go to people's homes. They feed and play with the pets.

ACTIVITY

WATCH, LEARN, AND DO

Many pet stores have pet groomers. See if your local pet store has this service. Go to the pet store. Ask pet store workers if you can watch the groomers at work. What tasks do the groomers do? What pets do they work with?

If you have a pet, ask your parents about how it stays clean. Perhaps you can help give your dog a bath. Or you can brush out your cat's fur.

FURTHER RESOURCES

Want to know more about pet grooming?
Learn more here:

Animal Behavior College Blog: How to Become a Dog Groomer
www.animalbehaviorcollege.com/blog/how-to-become-a-dog-groomer/

Animal Planet: The World of Creative Dog Grooming Exists
www.animalplanet.com/tv-shows/preposterous-pets/videos/the-world-of-
creative-dog-grooming-exists

Doctors Foster and Smith: Dog Brush Selection Guide
www.drsfostersmith.com/pic/article.cfm?articleid=248

Curious about different dog breeds?
Check out these sources:

American Kennel Club: Dog Breeds
www.akc.org/dog-breeds/

Gagne, Tammy. *West Highlands, Scotties, and Other Terriers*. North Mankato,
Minn.: Capstone, 2017.

INDEX